DATE DUE 1 /02

GAYLORD			PRINTED IN U.S.A.

CHECKERBOARD NATURE LIBRARY

INSECTS

Mosquitoes

by Cari Meister

ABDO

visit us at
www.abdopub.com

Published by ABDO Publishing Company, 4940 Viking Drive, Suite 622, Edina, Minnesota 55435. Copyright © 2001 Abdo Consulting Group, Inc., Pentagon Tower, P.O. Box 36036, Minneapolis, Minnesota 55435 USA. International copyrights reserved in all countries. No part of this book may be reproduced in any form without written permission from the publisher.

Printed in the United States

Illustrators: Edwin Beylerian, Carey Molter

Cover photo: Corbis Images

Interior photos: Animals Animals, Artville, Corel, Corbis Images, Peter Arnold, Inc., PhotoDisc, PictureQuest

Editors: Tamara L. Britton, Kate A. Furlong

Design and production: MacLean & Tuminelly

Library of Congress Cataloging-in-Publication Data

Meister, Cari.
　　Mosquitoes / Cari Meister.
　　　　p. cm. -- (Insects)
　　ISBN 1-57765-464-1
　　　1. Mosquitoes--Juvenile literature. [1. Mosquitoes.] I. Title.

　QL536 .M36 2000
　595.77'2--dc21

00-056880

Contents

What is a Mosquito?

Mosquitoes are interesting members of the insect world. They have been buzzing around Earth for millions of years. Long ago, mosquitoes fed on dinosaur blood! Today, they feast on human and animal blood.

There are about 2,500 different kinds of mosquitoes on Earth. They live all over the globe. Mosquitoes can be annoying to humans. But they are an important source of food for many other animals.

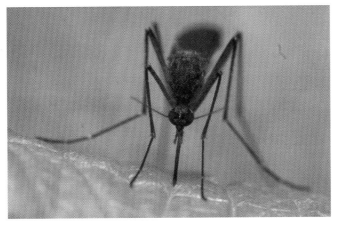

A mosquito sucking blood from a person.

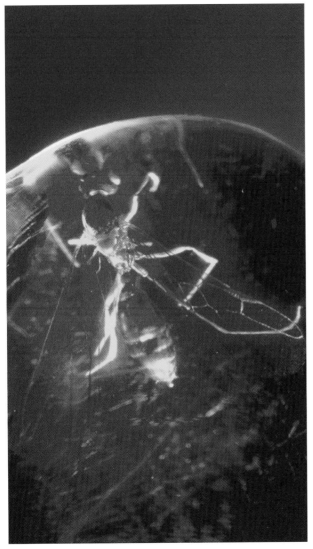

This mosquito was preserved in amber.

Most mosquitoes are harmless. But, some mosquitoes carry diseases that can be deadly. Scientists have worked hard to stop these diseases from spreading.

The Mosquito's Body

A mosquito's body is divided into three parts. These three parts are the head, thorax, and abdomen. A mosquito has a round head with large eyes. Behind the head lies the thorax. It has a pair of wings. It also has the mosquito's six long, skinny legs. Behind the thorax lies the abdomen. It holds the mosquito's organs.

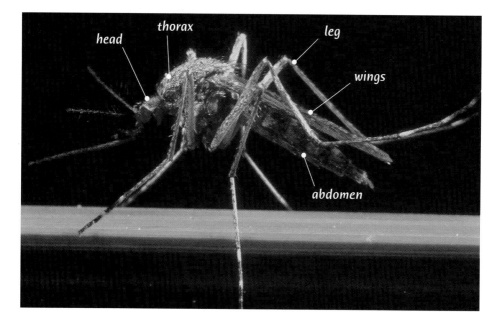

6

Male mosquitoes look different than females. Male mosquitoes have bushy **antennae** and long **palps**. Females also have antennae and palps. But their antennae are not as bushy. And, their palps are not as long.

Male mosquitoes have bushy antennae.

All mosquitoes have a long proboscis. They use the proboscis to suck plant nectar. A female mosquito has special mouthparts in its proboscis. These mouthparts can pierce skin and suck blood. Only female mosquitoes suck blood. They need blood to nourish their eggs.

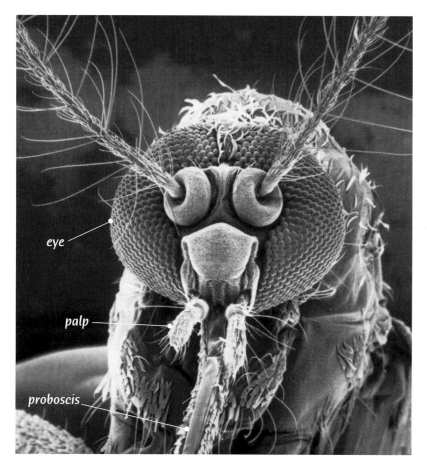

eye

palp

proboscis

Mosquitoes have many organs inside their bodies. Each organ has a different job. The brain acts as a control center. The heart pumps blood. The gut digests food.

Mosquitoes also have muscles inside their bodies. Muscles help them move and fly. Mosquitoes are fast fliers. Their wings can beat 500–600 times in one second! The buzzing sound a mosquito makes is really the sound of its wings flapping.

Mosquitoes do not have bones to protect their organs. Instead, mosquitoes have exoskeletons. They are hard, outer casings.

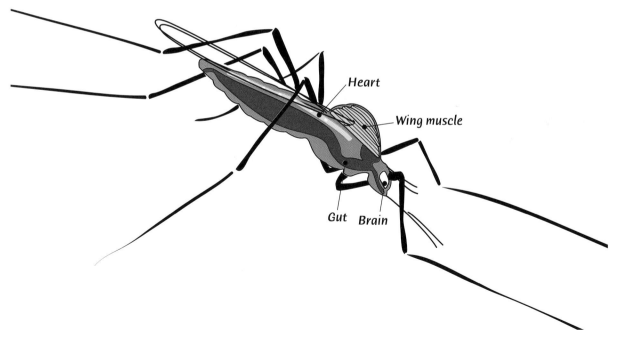

Heart

Wing muscle

Gut   Brain

How They Grow

A mosquito's life has four stages. The stages are egg, larva, pupa, and adult. All mosquitoes begin life as an egg. Female mosquitoes lay eggs in water such as ponds, rivers, swamps, or puddles. A mosquito may lay between 100 and 400 eggs at a time. The eggs float on top of the water in a clump called a raft.

In three days, the eggs develop into larvae. Mosquito larvae are called *wrigglers* because they are always swimming.

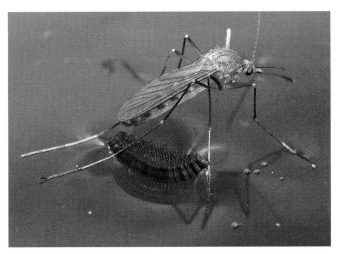

A female mosquito laying eggs.

Wrigglers look like long, clear worms. They hang upside down from the water by tubes called siphons. Siphons allow the wrigglers to breathe. Wrigglers eat tiny animals and plants. As they grow, wrigglers shed their skin about four times. This takes about two weeks.

When wrigglers shed their skin for the last time, they turn into pupae. Mosquito pupae are called *tumblers* because they tumble around in the water. Mosquitoes remain tumblers for about two days. During this time, they begin to grow into adult mosquitoes.

Mosquito larvae are called wrigglers.

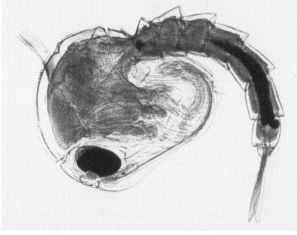

A mosquito pupa growing into an adult.

Once the tumbler has grown into an adult, it breaks through its skin. At first it's wet and cannot fly. It waits on the water's surface until its body dries and hardens. Then it is able to fly off and begin its life as an adult mosquito.

What They Eat

Mosquitoes use their palps and antennae to find food. Most mosquitoes eat plant nectar. Female mosquitoes also feed on blood from humans and animals.

Most mosquitoes eat plant nectar.

A female mosquito can easily detect her prey, even in the dark. That's because she senses every breath it takes. When a human or animal breathes, it lets out a gas called carbon dioxide. A mosquito's palps sense the gas. A mosquito can also find her prey by sensing its movement and body heat.

12

Once a female finds her prey, she pierces its skin with her proboscis. She uses her proboscis to find a small blood tube called a capillary. Once she finds a capillary, she injects saliva into it. This thins the blood and makes it easier for her to suck.

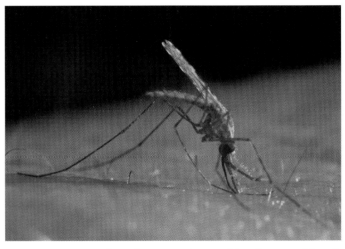

A female mosquito sucking human blood.

A female mosquito with blood in her abdomen.

A mosquito feasts on her prey for about 90 seconds. She stores the blood in her abdomen, which quickly becomes red and swollen. After she has finished eating, she flies away.

13

Where They Live

Mosquitoes live everywhere in the world except the open sea, the driest deserts, and the **poles**. Mosquitoes make their homes near rivers, ponds, lakes, pools, or other bodies of water. Most mosquitoes like to live in areas with **damp**, warm weather.

Mosquitoes have very short lives. They usually live about two weeks. Because they have such short lives, mosquitoes do not travel far. Females usually stay close to water so they can lay their eggs.

Mosquitoes like to live near water.

14

A mosquito and a drop of dew on a blade of grass.

Enemies

Mosquitoes have many natural enemies. Bats, birds, frogs, newts, beetles, and fish eat mosquitoes. Water scorpions and other underwater predators eat mosquito eggs, larvae, and pupae.

Bats, birds, and frogs are all enemies of the mosquito.

People are also enemies of the mosquito. In some areas, people drain shallow water so the mosquitoes have no place to lay their eggs. People spray chemicals in the air to kill adult mosquitoes. And they put other chemicals in the water to kill eggs, larvae, and pupae. The chemicals kill the mosquitoes. But they kill other plants and animals, too.

This plane is spraying chemicals to kill mosquitoes.

Mosquitoes & People

Mosquitoes are more dangerous to humans than any other insect. They pick up diseases easily. All they have to do is bite a sick person or animal. Once they have picked up the disease, they pass it on to other animals and people through their saliva. These diseases can harm and even kill people. Most of the mosquitoes in North America are annoying but harmless.

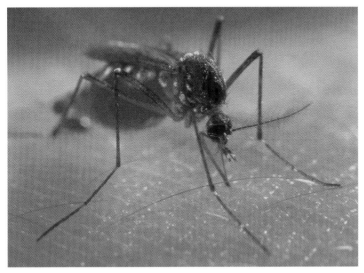

A mosquito sucks blood from human skin.

The diseases carried by mosquitoes almost stopped the Panama Canal from being built. In 1904, William Gorgas solved the problem. He drained swamps around the canal so mosquitoes could not lay eggs. He put screens on windows and nets around beds to protect the workers from mosquitoes. Gorgas's plans kept the workers healthy, and the canal was completed in 1914.

This person wears netting and uses bug spray to keep mosquitoes away.

Fun Facts

 Mosquitoes do not bite. The itchy, red bump you get after a mosquito feasts on you is caused by an allergic reaction to the mosquito's saliva.

 Mosquitoes can detect an animal or person from 40 yards (37 m) away, even in the dark!

 Mosquitoes are closely related to black flies and midges.

Black flies are closely related to mosquitoes.

There are about 100 trillion mosquitoes in the world today.

You can help control mosquitoes near your home. Do not leave standing water around during mosquito mating season. Empty watering cans, buckets, and birdbaths so that mosquitoes do not have a place to lay their eggs.

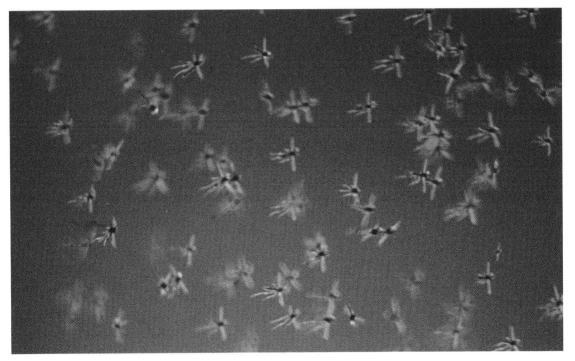

A swarm of mosquitoes.

Glossary

antennae – sense organs attached to the top of an insect's head.

capillary – a very tiny blood vessel.

damp – slightly wet.

exoskeleton – the outer casing that protects an insect.

inject – to force fluid through the skin.

larva – the stage of an insect's life that comes between hatching and pupa. Larvae are usually long and wormlike.

nectar – a sweet liquid formed in many flowers.

nourish – to give food to something.

palps – sense organs.

Panama Canal – a canal that connects the Atlantic and Pacific oceans.

poles – either end of Earth's axis; the North or South Pole.

predator – an animal that eats and/or kills other animals.

prey – animals that are eaten by predators.

proboscis – an insect's tubelike mouthparts; used for sucking and piercing.

pupa – the stage of an insect's life that comes between larva and adult.

raft – a floating group of mosquito eggs.

saliva – a liquid that keeps the mouth moist.

Web Sites

http://www.ex.ac.uk/bugclub/
  Join the Bug Club! This site for young entomologists
  includes a newsletter, puzzles and games.

http://www.epa.gov/pesticides/citizens/mosquito.htm
  This informative site by the Environmental Protection
  Agency teaches about diseases mosquitoes carry, their
  life cycle, and how to fight them.

http://www–rci.rutgers.edu/~insects/mosbiol.htm
  This site sponsored by Rutgers University has video clips
  of mosquitoes and detailed diagrams of the mosquito's
  body.

Index